Find a Job in Australia

Find a Job in Australia

by

NADINE MYERS

Second Edition

Internet addresses and Australian immigration information given in this book were accurate at the time it went to press.

www.nadinemyers.com

DISCLAIMER
While every effort has been made by the author to present accurate and up to date information in this book, it is apparent that internet addresses and Australian migration rules rapidly change; and therefore, the author reserves the right to update the contents and information provided here in as these changes progress. The author takes no responsibility for any errors or omissions if such discrepancies exist within this document.

Any results obtained by readers following the instruction in this book will vary based on individual application of the contents herein, the individual's consistency and dedication to their job search, as well as their efforts in keeping up to date with Australian migration rules as they apply to the individual. Thus, no guarantees can be made accurately, and therefore, no guarantees are made.

Where links are present, it is possible that they may change or even not work for many reasons beyond the control of the author and/or distributors. Furthermore, the author cannot guarantee or otherwise be responsible for what you might find when you click through to sites not under the control of the publisher of this book.

It is the reader's sole responsibility to seek professional advice before taking any action on their part.

ISBN: **1500597392**
ISBN-13: 978-1500597399

Printed in USA

Find a Job in Australia

By

NADINE MYERS

DEDICATION

This book is dedicated to all of the people I have worked with who have found employment in Australia from overseas, against all odds. You continue to be an inspiration to me and to others.

Also by Nadine Myers

Find Sponsored Jobs in Australia

Find Jobs in Oz: A Job Search Guide for PR Holders

Australian Resumes: Steps to Creating an Effective Australian Resume

Australian Cover Letters: Steps to Creating an Effective Australian Cover Letter

CVs for Job Sponsorship in Australia

LinkedIn Strategy for Job Search

Contents

Introduction

"Your success is measured by the strength of your desire; the size of your dream; and how you handle disappointment along the way."

- Robert Kiyosaki

This book was developed to help you start on your path to finding a job in Australia – whether you already have PR or a Working Holiday Visa (WHV), whether you've only just decided you'd like to look into migrating to Australia, or whether you need employer sponsorship in order to migrate.

I know how difficult it is for people who dream to live in Australia to make their dream a reality, because not everyone knows just how they can make it happen.

There are definitely some secrets to successfully landing a job in Australia, and we touch on some of these in this book.

This book will not only help you determine whether you qualify to migrate to Australia, but also prepare you for applying for jobs in Australia, as well as help you to develop a successful job search strategy to ensure that you are doing all you can to secure employment in Australia.

This is a great introductory book to help you on your way, and touches on the following topics:

- ✓ *Finding out your visa options*
- ✓ *Preparing your CV for Australia*
- ✓ *Writing a compelling cover letter*
- ✓ *Planning your job search*
- ✓ *Developing a job search strategy*
- ✓ *Using job search websites & recruitment agencies*
- ✓ *Migration expos*
- ✓ *The hidden job market*
- ✓ *Getting job-ready*

We will also look at some case studies and success stories from people who found employment in Australia, and the strategies they used, as well as their tips to you for getting started on the road to success.

I have set this book out to showcase the key points that you will need to consider when applying for jobs in Australia and how to be successful in your endeavours to secure employment. You will learn what some of the secrets to finding a job in Australia are, and also WHY they are necessary for landing a job in Australia. *This will allow you to take a completely new approach to your Australian job search and your job applications, and put you solidly on the road to success.*

Again, this book is just an introduction, and will only briefly look at some strategies that my in-depth books and mentoring courses at www.nadinemyers.com go into in greater detail; however it will certainly point you in the right direction for your Australian job search.

I believe you're worth that job and life that you really want in Australia, and I can't wait to assist you to achieve it!

Migration Streams

"The ladder of success is best climbed by stepping on the rungs of opportunity."

- Ayn Rand

What Visa Do I Qualify For?

Many people spend months applying for jobs in Australia, only to discover down the track that they do not actually qualify for migrating to Australia.

This can be heart breaking, especially after spending months searching and putting loads of energy and time into the task of finding a job.

Not only that, but the *rules for migration are changing constantly* – at least once per year; with many occupations no longer in demand and therefore being removed from the list of occupations that qualify, whilst other occupations appear that weren't there previously.

It is therefore *crucial*, as a first step, to find out your status for migrating to Australia; and staying on top of the immigration rules so that you can be confident at all times what you qualify for.

A professional migration assessment is the best way to find out if and what Australian visa/s you qualify for. We will look at professional migration assessments in the next section.

Professional Migration Assessments

The safest way to discover whether you qualify for employer sponsorship in Australia, and to avoid an incorrect conclusion, is to book a professional assessment with a registered and knowledgeable migration agent.

The reason this is more effective is because they are *trained*, *qualified* and *experienced* in assessing overseas nationals to determine whether they qualify for a visa for Australia.

Registered migration agents are also **up-to-date** on all the changes in rules that seem to occur on a regular basis these days. **At least once per year** there is a review of the occupations that are in demand in Australia**,** and the skilled occupation lists are adjusted accordingly, often meaning that many occupations are removed from the lists.

A few years ago a migration agent told me that there are more than 100 types of visas for Australia - I had no idea there were that many!

I urge you to be careful when selecting a migration agent to use, as there are many agents out there who claim to be migration agents, however, many are not qualified and/or registered with the Australian Department of Immigration.

Only migration agents who are registered with the Australian government are authorised by law to provide migration advice for Australia.

A few things to keep in mind when selecting a suitable migration agent are set out below:

- As mentioned, check that the agent is registered with MARA

- Check their fees (you can find out here what they should be charging: www.mara.gov.au/using-an-agent/working-with-your-agent/agent-fees/)

- Research the agent on Google and seek out testimonials

- Some agents will give you their success rate, which can give you confidence

Using an agent that comes highly recommended by someone you know - someone who has experience using that agent - is another great way to select a reputable migration agent.

It is very important that you *always check* that the migration agent you select is registered.

You can check whether your migration agent is registered, by following these steps:

1. Go to: **http://www.Mara.gov.au**   (Migration   Agents   Registration Authority)

2. Click on "Find an Agent"

3. Enter the agent's Name and Location, and if you have it you can also enter their business name for a more refined search

If you cannot find your migration agent on the MARA list, your agent is not registered with the Australian Government, and therefore should not be used.

If you do not currently have a migration agent, we can recommend our preferred migration agent to assist you, **TSS Immigration**. See the **Where to Next** chapter for full contact details.

Video: Selecting a Migration Agent

This video was produced by the Australian Government, to help you to make the right decision when selecting a migration agent to use, and is therefore helpful for you to watch.

https://youtu.be/CqPgNruY-lY

ACTION POINTS:

1. Decide upon a migration agent to use by following the advice in this section.

2. Check that your selected agent is registered with MARA.

3. Book for a professional migration assessment.

Doing Your Own Research

If you opt to do your own research to determine whether you qualify for migrating to Australia, I recommend that you be extremely thorough.

Since you won't have a migration agent advising you, you will need to ensure that you **regularly check** the Australian immigration site (www.border.gov.au) to stay up to date with the many changes that occur. This is important because you may find that one day you determine that you qualify for migrating to Australia, whereas the next day *rules may change* and you no longer qualify.

Qualifying Occupations

One place you can start with your research is to see whether your work experience and qualifications match an occupation that falls under the '*Qualifying Occupations*' for skilled migration to Australia. The steps for doing research in this area are set out below.

Step 1 – Qualifying Occupations

Reviewing the list of occupations that currently qualify for skilled migration is quite a simple process; although you will need to check back on these pages regularly to ensure you have current and up-to-date information.

Skilled Occupation List

The current **Skilled Occupation List** (SOL) is relevant for applicants for:

- Independent points-based skilled migration who are not nominated by a State or Territory Government agency

- A Family Sponsored Points Tested visa

- A Temporary Graduate visa (subclass 485) – Graduate Work stream.

Go through the SOL in its entirety, and write down the names of the occupations that you may qualify for, together with their respective ANZSCO codes.

You can view the SOL here:

http://www.border.gov.au/Trav/Work/Work/Skills-assessment-and-assessing-authorities/skilled-occupations-lists/SOL

Step 2 – Job Descriptions

Once you can see that there is one, or perhaps more, occupations that you MIGHT qualify for, you then need to review the job descriptions as set out by ANZSCO (www.abs.gov.au) to discover whether the job descriptions match your actual experience. To start the search, go to:

http://bit.ly/TLrFVX

Step 3 – Specifications of Each Occupation

On the above web page, enter the occupation title into the search box, with the ANZSCO codes you noted from the SOL. For example, "*234411 GEOLOGIST*". You then simply click on the "Go" button next to the search box.

When the search is complete, the page will offer you suggestions of occupation groups that your search might fit into. Click on the appropriate link offered. In the above example it would be: *2344, GEOLOGISTS AND GEOPHYSICISTS*.

You will then be taken to a page that gives you a description of what qualifications and specific experience you require to qualify for this occupation.

Be sure to study this page carefully, particularly the sections that apply to your specific occupation. This will ensure that you make a more accurate assessment of whether you qualify or not.

It may be helpful to print this page out so you can highlight the skills and experience that you do have as well as those that you don't have.

Step 4 – Skilled Migration or Sponsorship?

If you find one or more occupations that you may qualify for on the SOL, there is a very good chance that you will qualify for skilled migration.

Further, if your research in Step 3 has shown that you fit the majority of the criteria for one or more of the occupations you have noted; it is likely that you do *indeed* qualify for skilled migration.

You can then do additional research relevant to the skilled migration stream here:

http://www.border.gov.au/Trav/Work/Work/Skills-assessment-and-assessing-authorities/skilled-occupations-lists

If you *cannot* find an occupation that matches your background on the SOL, perhaps you do not qualify for skilled migration, and you will therefore need to look into *Employer Sponsorship*. I will help you get started in the upcoming sections.

If, after studying the job descriptions, you are still unsure whether you qualify for migrating to Australia, it is recommended that you book a professional assessment with a registered migration agent, such as TSS Immigration (please refer to the *Where to Next* section of this book for contact details).

This way you will be sure of whether to pursue your dream or to change direction in your life.

In the next course unit, we will look at how to research the various visas that are available to you in Australia.

ACTION POINTS:

1. Follow the steps above to do your own research into whether you qualify to migrate to Australia under the Skilled Migration Scheme.

2. If you aren't sure whether you qualify, book an assessment with a migration agent.

3. If you are confident that you qualify, make note of which occupation/s are relevant, and stay tuned for the next steps in the research process.

4. If you can't find any occupations that fit your background on the SOL, stay tuned for the upcoming section on finding out whether you qualify for employer sponsorship.

Further Visa Research

If you're *still* not sure where you stand for migrating to Australia, it can be helpful to use the **Visa Finder** tool on the Australian Immigration website.

The *Visa Finder* tool will help you to narrow down the types of visas you might qualify for, so you can then do further research into those particular visas to find out the criteria and requirements for those visas or visa.

To use the *Visa Finder* tool, follow these steps:

1.   Go to the Australian Immigration website, **www.border.gov.au**

2.   Under "Individuals & Travellers", click on "Visas"

3.   Complete the details in the Visa Finder tool and click on "Find a Visa"

Review your results, as you should have been offered some potential visas that you may qualify for based on the answers you provided regarding your circumstances.

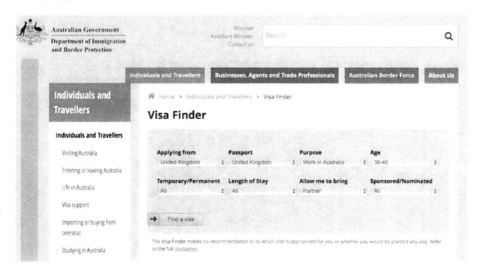

As an example, in the above screenshot you can see that I filled out the *Visa Finder* form stating that I am:

- From the UK;

- Holding a UK Passport;

- Having the purpose to work in Australia;

- Aged 36-40;

- Looking at All Temporary or Permanent visa types;

- Looking at All lengths of stay;

- Wanting to bring my partner with me; and

- Looking at All Sponsored/Nominated Visas

This search turned back a result of 19 visa types, including:

- Temporary Work (Skilled) visa (subclass 457)

- Skilled Independent visa (subclass 189)

- Business Innovation and Investment (Permanent) visa (subclass 888)

- Temporary Work (Long Stay Activity) visa (subclass 401)

- Business Talent (Permanent) visa (subclass 132)

- Temporary Work (Short Stay Activity) visa (subclass 400)

- Business Innovation and Investment (Provisional) visa (subclass 188)

- Employer Nomination Scheme (subclass 186)

- Skilled Nominated visa (subclass 190)

- Distinguished Talent visa (subclass 124)

- Regional Sponsored Migration Scheme visa (subclass 187)

- Temporary Work (International Relations) visa (subclass 403)

- Temporary Work (Entertainment) visa (subclass 420)

- Skilled Regional (Provisional) visa (subclass 489)

- Business Owner visa (subclass 890)

- Investor visa (subclass 891)

- State/Territory Sponsored Business Owner visa (subclass 892)

- State/Territory Sponsored Investor visa (subclass 893)

- Maritime Crew visa (subclass 988)

You can find brief information on each visa on the results page, as you can see in the below example, as well as links to do further research on each visa.

After researching each visa that comes up in your search, you should be able to narrow these down to visas that meet your requirements for living and working in Australia, and you should also be able to learn whether you meet the criteria for those visas. Once you have decided which visa you want to apply for, follow the links to find out how you go about applying for those types of visas so you can make the necessary preparations.

Take note that the results that you turn out from your search **do not** necessarily mean that you qualify for those visas. Rather, the results indicate that it is a **possibility** that you may for those visas. Please see the disclaimer:

The Visa Finder makes no recommendation as to which visa is appropriate for you or whether you would be granted any visa. Refer to the full disclaimer: http://www.border.gov.au/website/copyright-and-disclaimer.

Again, if you're not sure about which visa/s you might qualify for, I recommend that you book a professional migration assessment.

ACTION POINTS:

1. Follow the steps to find out what visas you qualify, by using the Australian Immigration Visa Finder at www.border.gov.au.

2. Follow the links to do further research into the visas that come up in your search, and find out whether you meet the criteria.

3. Once you have determined which visa you should qualify for, and that suits your requirements in terms of living and working in Australia, it is time to do additional research into what is required to apply.

Expression of Interest / SkillSelect

Expression of Interest (EOI) is a relatively new way to apply for skilled migration to Australia, which is done through a system called *SkillSelect*.

If you are interested in the points-based skilled migration or business investment and innovation visa program, you are now required to submit an EOI and receive an invitation before you can lodge a visa application.

It is beneficial for you to read this section, even if you believe you are not interested in the above types of visas, as this may be an option for you even if you are seeking employer sponsorship (more on employer sponsorship in the next section).

SkillSelect

SkillSelect is an online service enabling skilled workers and business people interested in migrating to Australia to submit their details so that they can be considered for a skilled visa via an 'Expression of Interest' or 'EOI'.

The SkillSelect program came into force on 1 July 2012, meaning that any skilled persons wanting to migrate to Australia will need to submit their details first through SkillSelect, as an EOI; and then will need to wait to be invited before they can apply for one of the new points tested skilled migration visas.

This program is very similar to the online submission program that has been in effect in New Zealand for some time; which in an indication that this process for applying for skilled migration is an effective one.

SkillSelect came about to ensure that the skilled migration program is based on the "economic needs of Australia", and to instil greater controls on who can apply for skilled migration, when they can apply, and how many people can apply in any given year.

Applicable Visas

The following visas must be applied for following submission of a *successful EOI* through SkillSelect:

- Business Talent (Permanent) visa (subclass 132)

- Business Innovation and Investment (Provisional) visa (subclass 188)

- Skilled Independent visa (subclass 189)

- Skilled – Nominated visa (subclass 190)

- Skilled – Nominated or Sponsored (Provisional) visa (subclass 489).

The following three visas can be applied for following an invitation by a SkillSelect-approved Australian employer:

- Temporary Work (Skilled) visa (subclass 457)

- Employer Nomination Scheme visa (subclass 186)

- Regional Sponsored Migration Scheme visa (subclass 187).

Although it is not necessary for you to submit an EOI for the last visas listed above, by doing so you will **open opportunities for Australian employers to find your details and contact you / nominate you for a visa**.

Benefits

The bonus of this program is that processing times for visas are expected to decrease, meaning you should have your visa even sooner than previously.

Likely, as the trend has been moving, there will be more opportunities in regional areas than in major cities – you should therefore keep this in mind and the more you are open to regional areas of Australia to live and work, the more chance you will have in gaining a visa (if you meet all requirements of the visa).

This program will also mean that opportunities may be opened for you to be *found* and *nominated* for skilled visas by Australian employers, or you may be *invited* by the Australian Government to lodge a visa application.

Your EOI will stay in the system for a period of *two years*. During this time, you can *update your application* with additional work experience and qualifications, among other things; allowing you to obtain extra points toward your visa.

You are able to *withdraw* your application during this two year period, should your circumstances change; and your application will be withdrawn automatically if you are granted a visa.

Applying From Within Australia

You should note that submitting an EOI from within Australia does not grant you a bridging visa, as it is not a visa application.

If you are invited to apply for a visa, and you are in Australia at the time, you must be in Australia lawfully (holding a substantive visa or a Bridging Visa A or B) for you to be granted a visa.

Please note that anyone can submit an EOI, however, you must meet the necessary visa requirements for the visa(s) you are expressing an interest in. If it is a requirement for your visa that you have completed an *English Language Test*, *Skills Assessment* or *Job Ready Program*, and you haven't, then **you cannot submit an EOI**.

NB – If you give false information on your EOI, and after you are invited to apply for your visa (s) are found to not meet the requirements; **your visa will be refused**. Not only that, your information provided may be considered fraud, which could subject you to a three year ban, which may in turn prevent the grant of a further visa.

To learn more about SkillSelect and EOI, visit:

http://www.border.gov.au/Trav/Work/Skil

ACTION POINTS:

1. Do some research into the EOI / SkillSelect program to find out whether this is the route you should take for applying for a visa for Australia.

2. If you are still unsure as to what visa/s you qualify for in Australia, I recommend that you consult a migration agent, such as TSS Immigration (see the section called, '*Where to Next*' for details of how to contact TSS Immigration).

Employer Sponsorship

Employer Sponsorship is where an approved Australian company sponsors you for employment in Australia, and in doing so, you receive a visa that allows you to migrate to Australia under the condition that you remain employed by the company who has sponsored you.

You should note that this **doesn't necessarily mean that all costs are covered** by the company; in some cases they are, and in other cases, you will have to cover your portion of the visa costs and your relocation costs.

What it does mean when you are sponsored by a company is that you are given the rights to come out and live in Australia for the duration of the visa, because a company is offering you a job.

In the majority of cases, the visa that you receive is a temporary visa, meaning that you can only live and work in Australia for the duration of the visa. However, this is a very attractive option for skilled overseas nationals, as it often means they can migrate to Australia sooner than if they had applied for Permanent Residency (skilled migration). It is often also the only option available to many people, who may not qualify for other types of migrant visas.

As mentioned previously, it is recommended that before you start your search for jobs in Australia, you should *first determine that you qualify* for migrating – this is also true for applying for employer sponsored jobs in Australia.

Some people believe that if they do not qualify for General Skilled Migration, that their only option is employer sponsorship or 457 visas sponsorship. While this is true in some cases, in many cases, people do not even qualify for this type of visa. It is therefore highly recommended that you do all of the necessary research to uncover whether you do indeed qualify for employer sponsorship, especially if you have determined that you don't qualify for skilled migration.

Types of Employer Sponsorship

As with researching whether you qualify for skilled migration, if you opt to do your own research to discover whether you qualify for employer sponsorship, you need to be extremely thorough and ensure that you regularly check back to the Australian immigration site (www.border.gov.au) to stay up to date with the changes that occur.

There are two types of employer sponsorship in Australia. The first is **Skilled Workers Temporary**; which includes:

- 457 Visas (standard business sponsorship)

The second type is **Skilled Workers Permanent** Visas, including:

- Employer Nomination Scheme (ENS 186)
- Regional Sponsored Migration Scheme (RSMS 187)

There is also the Expression of Interest (EOI) programme, which is submitted via the online SkillSelect service (as covered in the previous section).

Australian immigration rules are changing regularly, so we recommend that you keep up to date with what's happening with Australian sponsorship visas, at the Australian immigration website: http://www.border.gov.au.

Many people do not understand the main differences between the types of employer sponsored visas, and as such, do not want to be considered for temporary sponsorship visas. *This is decision does not go in a potential migrant's favour.*

It should be understood that many companies in Australia **prefer temporary sponsorship** due to the lower risk factor; that being, if the sponsored employee does not work out, the company is not obliged to keep them employed past their visa expiration date.

In comparison, although the permanent visa is more attractive to the person being sponsored, the employer actually takes a rather large risk in hiring someone on a permanent basis whom they have often never meet before, nor seen perform in the workplace; and therefore their preference is to opt for the temporary visa, at least to start with. If the sponsored employee proves themselves worthy, the company will in some cases assist them to achieve their Permanent Residency through sponsorship.

The rules for permanent sponsorship visas are much stricter than for temporary visas; and more often than not, you will not qualify for the permanent visa. Sometimes, you may not qualify for either – it is best to find out (more on this shortly).

Do to the temporary sponsorship visa being the preferred visa type for Australian employers, I urge you to consider temporary visa sponsorship. Even though the risk may appear greater at your end - being that if the company does not sponsor your PR you will need to find another employer sponsor or leave the country - you will more likely have the opportunity to migrate to Australia on a temporary visa, as permanent sponsorship is almost impossible to find.

How to Find Out if You Qualify

There are a two ways that you can uncover whether you do indeed qualify for employer sponsorship in Australia, and these are:

1. Take a professional assessment with a registered migration agent; or

2. Do your own research using the Australian immigration websites.

Many people make the decision to do their own research because they do not want to pay for the migration agent fees; however, if they are not thorough enough, they may make an error in their self-assessment, and find out in the 'last hour' that all their time and efforts have been in vain.

I therefore recommend that you take a **professional migration assessment** to receive an accurate assessment of your options.

Taking a Migration Assessment

As mentioned previous sections, the safest way to discover whether you qualify for any type of visa in Australia, including employer sponsorship, and to avoid an incorrect self-assessment, is to have a professional assessment with a registered and knowledgeable migration agent.

Please refer to the previous section on selecting a **migration agent**.

Doing Your Own Research

If you opt to do your own research to determine whether you qualify for employer sponsorship in Australia – like with researching other visas – be extremely thorough and ensure that you regularly check back to the Australian immigration site (www.border.gov.au) to stay up to date with the immigration rules.

Doing your own research to find out whether you qualify for employer sponsorship in Australia is the same method as described in the previous section. However, in case you skipped the previous section and have come straight to this section to find out whether you qualify for employer sponsorship, I have set out the steps below for your research.

Step 1 – Qualifying Occupations

The first place you can start is by reviewing the list of occupations that currently qualify for employer sponsorship. The list that is relevant for employer sponsorship visas is the *Consolidated Sponsored Occupation List* (CSOL).

Again – be sure to check on these pages regularly as the list changes frequently.

Consolidated Sponsored Occupation List:

The current CSOL is relevant for applicants for:

- Points-based skilled migration who are nominated by a state or territory government agency under a State Migration Plan

- The Employer Nomination Scheme (ENS), who must have been nominated by an Australian employer to fill a position in an occupation that appears in the CSOL

- Temporary Work (Skilled) visa (subclass 457)

- Training and Research visa (subclass 402)

You can view the CSOL here:

http://www.border.gov.au/Trav/Work/Work/Skills-assessment-and-assessing-authorities/skilled-occupations-lists/CSOL

For Updates on Employer Sponsorship, visit: http://www.border.gov.au

Step 2 – Job Descriptions

Once you can see that there is one, or perhaps more, occupations that you MIGHT qualify for, you need to review the job descriptions as set out by ANZSCO (www.abs.gov.au) to discover whether the job descriptions match your actual experience. To start the search, go to:

http://bit.ly/TLrFVX

Step 3 – Specifications Of Each Occupation

On the above web page, enter the occupation title into the search box, with the ANZSCO codes if possible (you will find these next to the relevant jobs on the CSOL above). For example, "234411 Geologist". You then simply click on the "Go" button next to the search box.

When the search is complete, the page will offer you a suggestion of an occupation group that your search might fit into. Click on the appropriate link offered. In the above example it would be: *2344, Geologists and Geophysicists.*

You will then be taken to a page that gives a description of what qualifications and specific experience you require to qualify for this occupation.

Be sure to study this page carefully, particularly the sections that apply to your specific occupation. This will ensure that you make a more accurate assessment of whether you qualify or not.

Think You Qualify?

If after your research, you are confident that you qualify for employer sponsorship, and that is the visa route you are going to focus on, you are now ready to prepare yourself for the Australian job market! The modules following will help you to get started.

I always recommend, however, that you verify this with a **registered migration agent**, for peace of mind that you are indeed correct. It will be money well spent.

Not Sure You Qualify?

If, after studying the job descriptions, you are still unsure that you qualify, it is recommended that you book a professional assessment with a registered migration agent, such as TSS Immigration (see the section "*Where to Next*" for contact details for TSS Immigration).

By verifying with a migration agent, you will then be sure of whether to pursue your dream or to change direction in your life.

One of the big advantages of consulting with a recommended MARA registered migration agent is that if it appears that you do not qualify for the Australian employer sponsorship programme, the agent can advise you, where applicable, of the 'pathways' you can take to meet the criteria required to qualify for employer sponsorship.

ACTION POINTS:

1. Follow the steps above to do your own research into whether you qualify to migrate to Australia under the employer sponsorship scheme.

2. If you aren't sure whether you qualify (and even if you are fairly sure), it is recommended that you book an assessment with a migration agent.

3. Once you have confirmed that you do qualify for employer sponsorship, and that this is the visa route you will be focusing on, get ready to prepare yourself for your job search (in the following sections of this book).

Marketing for Success

*"One important key to success is self-confidence.
An important key to self-confidence is preparation."*

- Arthur Ashe

Australian Resume / CV

Finding and securing a job in Australia, especially employer sponsorship, does not happen by luck. Although this may surprise you, it is actually good news, because it means that if everyone followed the same steps in the same way, they would have just as much chance as the next person, of finding a job in Australia.

If you follow all the same steps that other people who have had success have followed, in exactly the same way, you have just as much chance of finding a job in Australia!

There are several steps and strategies that you can implement that will dramatically increase your chance of landing a job in Australia.

The first step is ensuring your marketing materials are *strategically set up for success*. This is crucial to your job search, so whatever you do, do not assume that your current marketing materials are sufficient for finding a job in Australia. Always assume they are not – this way you will only benefit, as the worst case scenario is that you end up with a highly effective CV and cover letter for Australia – which are *essential for finding a job there*. Spend quality time on the next few tasks, and it will ensure you are right on track.

Marketing for an Australian Job

If you thought that you could just apply for jobs in Australia without making any effort with your marketing materials, you thought wrong.

Marketing is a great part of everything that we do. For example, if you started a new business and put no effort at all into your marketing and branding, do you think you would get any customers? Unlikely!

It works the same with looking for a job in Australia. Your *'business'* is finding a *'customer'* (i.e. an Australian employer) who will buy your *'product'* (i.e. your skills and experience) by hiring you.

Your potential *'customers'* will be looking at other *'products'* (i.e. candidates with similar experience) who are Australian residents (and therefore have Australian experience, so are regarded more highly), and these 'products' therefore are more attractive to the 'customer'.

As such, **you need to work even harder** so that your product can *compete* against these other products; and you can start by preparing your marketing documents for success.

You may have already put some effort into your marketing documents and are feeling really good about them. However, **what works well in your home country doesn't necessarily work well in Australia**, so it is always better to be sure that you are on the right path.

Start With Your Resume

If you are trying to sell a product to Italians, do you think you will get very far if you cannot speak to them in Italian? Probably not!

It is very important to **know what your market wants**, and to approach them in the most effective way that will *sell your product*. When selling a product to Italians, that means speaking in Italian. When selling your skills and experience to Australian employers, that means presenting your skills and experience in Australian language, and meeting the Australian employers' expectations.

In case you were unaware, Australian resumes (or CVs) are different from resumes in other countries. Not only that, but if you are seeking employer sponsorship or your first job in Australia, you need to go that one step further and make yourself stand out and compete as effectively as you can against local candidates who are in competition for the same job.

Create an Effective Australian CV

If you're not sure where to start with getting your resume into an effective Australian format, you can do some research on Google to see just how an Australian CV/Resume should be presented.

If you visit www.resumeaustralia.net, you can view high-impact CV templates that have proven to be successful in Australia, and you will get a good idea of how you should be aiming to make your own CV look, especially if you really want to stand out from other applicants (which you most definitely need to).

For full instructions on how to write an effective resume or CV for Australia, including templates you can use and a bonus cover letter book; I recommend the book, '*Australian Resumes: Steps to Creating an Effective Australian Resume*', which is available at Resume Australia (www.resumeaustralia.net).

Australian Resumes: Steps to Creating an Effective Australian Resume – available on Amazon, and at: www.resumeaustralia.net.

ACTION POINTS:

1. **Do research into how Australian resumes are presented, and start to make changes to your own resume so that it meets (or exceeds) the expectations of Australian employers.**

2. **Visit: www.resumeaustralia.net to view and download effective Australian resume templates, or check out the guide at: http://www.resumeaustralia.net/resume-cover-letter-ebooks.**

Do not move on to the next chapter until you have completed your **Australian CV**, as this is a crucial step towards the success of your Australian job search.

Once you have your Australian resume/CV in place, it is time to prepare your cover letter for success!

Australian Cover Letter

When applying for jobs with employer sponsorship in Australia, or your first job after receiving your PR or working visa, your cover letter is the second most important part of your overall job application (behind your resume), and in some cases, the most important.

A well-written cover letter that is straight to the point and relevant to the job you are applying for can act as an excellent support for your CV/resume. A poorly written cover letter can close the doors to your applications prematurely, especially if you do not, for example, approach your visa sponsorship requirement effectively.

A few key tips for writing a positively impacting cover letter for your situation are set out below.

Don't Write an Essay

One of the biggest mistakes that people make when applying for jobs in Australia is to write a cover letter that is **unnecessarily long**. Keep your cover letter *short* and *to the point* and aim for **half-to-one page in length**. Only include *relevant points* that support your application to the *specific* job you are applying for, and don't fill the letter with information that has nothing to do with the job that has been described.

Tailor Your Cover Letter to the Job You're Applying For

When you write your cover letter, it is OK to have a standard letter that you are sending out to a couple of different jobs. However, make sure that you *tailor the letter to each individual job* that you apply for.

A lot of people make the mistake of using the same letter over and over and this can lead to *embarrassing errors*, such as sending out letters that are addressed to the wrong person, that are referring to the wrong job title, and/or that are full of information that is not relevant to the job they are applying for. Make sure that you take care to check each letter before sending it out so that it is tailored to the specific job and company that is offering the position.

Address the Selection Criteria

If there are specific selection criteria the employer has stated in their job advert, or the advert refers to key attributes, skills and/or experience that the employer is looking for in their ideal candidate; then you should make sure that you **address how these specific items relate to yourself**.

Hiring managers are looking for those **key skills**; otherwise they wouldn't have listed them in their adverts. If you do not make the employer aware of your '*match*' to what they are looking for, you will likely not be considered for the position.

Further, when addressing the selection criteria in your cover letter; **back-up each of your statements** with a brief example. For instance, instead of stating, "*I am highly organised and work well to tight deadlines*"; support this statement with why, such as: "*I am highly organised and work well under pressure; and have demonstrated this in my previous roles through my adoption of techniques such as proper planning, prioritisation and delegation of work load where necessary*". **Now you are making a powerful statement against the selection criteria!**

Keep a Clear and Concise Layout

Just as in the case with your Australian CV/resume; when applying for jobs in Australia, your cover letter should be **clear**, **concise** and **to the point**. You need to keep in mind that hiring managers tend to scan CVs and cover letters for *key points* before going back to read the information in more detail (if they are inspired enough to do so).

Don't be afraid to highlight certain relevant points in **bold**, *italics* or even set out your strengths and examples against the job description in *bullet points* – this makes the information very easy to process when scanning the cover letter, and draws the reader's eye to the information that is important. Refrain from using long, drawn out descriptions, unless you are asked to address the selection criteria in a more comprehensive or formal manner, such as with Government applications. (Government applications are whole other topic, and require a more in-depth approach, which you will find in the book, '*Australian Cover Letters: Steps to Creating an Effective Australian Cover Letter*', available as a bonus with the book, '*Australian Resumes: Steps to Creating an Effective Australian Resume*', found at Resume Australia (www.resumeaustralia.net).

Australian Cover Letters: Steps to Creating an Effective Australian Cover Letter – available on Amazon, and at: www.resumeaustralia.net.

Formatting

The majority of hiring managers in Australia will appreciate a traditional letter format with your **name**, **address** and **contact number** and/or **Skype ID**, **email address**, their **company name**, **address** and the **name** of the correct person you are applying to all at the top. Then, underneath your address, start your letter with "*Dear Mr/Mrs/etc.*", selecting the relevant title and using their name if you have it; including a **subject heading** outlining the **job** you are applying for underneath, followed by the *body/content*, and finally, **signed off** by yourself. This shows *respect*, indicates that you *value presentation* and demonstrates your skill level with Word processing.

It is also acceptable to write your cover letter in an **email**, these days; however it shows more *effort* and *importance* if you take the time to write a *formal letter* as discussed above, and attach it as a Word document. Sometimes it's the *little things* that determine whether you are **screened out** or **short listed** for an interview.

Furthermore, where you can, use **Microsoft Word** documents for your cover letters (and Australian CV). The majority of Australian employers and recruiters do not have Apple devices, and although other programs may provide better-looking CVs and cover letters, your potential employer may not have that program available, and therefore will not be able to *open* your letter and CV; or worse – they can open the document/s but the formatting is showing up completely *out of sync*. This could mean an instant '*strike out*'! Microsoft Word is the *safest option* with all of your documents. Australian recruiters particularly prefer Word over PDF documents.

Spelling and Grammar

This may seem obvious; however, you should really take care with *spelling* and *grammar* in your job applications, particularly when you are from a *non-English* speaking country. This is even more so important when apply for jobs with *visa sponsorship* where written communication is important. If you can't illustrate that you can write a simple letter without making spelling mistakes and using incorrect grammar, you will make a *bad impression* from the start and may not get the opportunity to make up for it at the interview stage.

Always do *spelling* and *grammar* checks before sending your application, and where possible, have a trusted friend or family member run their eyes over your application before sending.

NB – Be sure to set your proofing language in MS Word to *Australian English*, so that you can ensure the correct Australian spelling and grammar in your cover letter and CV.

State What You're Looking For

Don't forget, when you're applying for a job with an organisation, you're also assessing *them* on whether they are the type of organisation *you* are looking for. By stating what kind of organisation you are ideally looking for, you are putting the 'ball back in the hiring manager's court' to assess whether they are up to *your* standards! **THIS CAN BE VERY POWERFUL**.

An example of this kind of statement is, "*I am ideally looking for a company that values its employees, and demonstrates this through supporting professional development, offering career progression or succession planning, having a flexible work place, and a friendly and positive working environment*". You could then follow up your statement with an *impression* you have received about this company possibly being on track with meeting your criteria, such as, "*from my research, company X appears to have this kind of culture, and I look forward to having the opportunity to learn more about your organisation and discussing this role in more detail*".

Your Availability

Always include your **availability** for attending *telephone / Skype* and/or *face-to-face interviews* for each role you are applying for. If done correctly, this can **increase** your chance of being considered for the role, especially if you show that you are prepared to attend serious interviews in Australia. The majority of employers will prefer to meet with potential employees **face-to-face** before hiring/sponsoring them (where possible), and being available in this regard may open more doors for you.

For *face-to-face* interviews, it is best if you can attend an interview **WITHIN 2 WEEKS**, or you may not be considered for an interview. Alternatively, you can state in your letter that you can *'attend a face-to-face interview with reasonable notice'*, indicating that the employer would have to be **reasonable** in allowing you to get organised with work and visas etc., in order to come out to Australia for an interview, without coming out and giving them a specific timeframe.

Further, you should also include your **availability to commence work** if the Australian employer decided to offer you a position. This means including your **notice period** with your current employer. Most employers will expect a notice period of around **one month**, so I recommend not making your notice period too much longer than this or this could also *'knock you out of the running'* of being considered for the role. After all, the employer wants to fill the position **now**, not three months or more into the future.

You may feel it appropriate at the beginning of the letter to state **why** you are now on the market for a new job – whether it is that you are *seeking new challenges*, or putting your *newly completed qualifications* to use etc. However, we advise that you **refrain** from stating your reason if it is that you have been *retrenched* or have had your job *terminated*. This can create a situation for conclusions to be reached before you have the opportunity to explain yourself – something you want to avoid.

Addressing the Sponsorship Requirement

If you are seeking a job that is offering **Employer Sponsorship**, there are *pros* and *cons* for including your visa status / sponsorship requirement on your covering letter. I have seen clients find employer sponsorship using **both** methods, so there really is not one preferred way to approach visa sponsorship. However, I will briefly cover both options here and leave the decision in your hands as to which you would feel more *comfortable* using. You may even like to experiment with both to uncover which is the most *effective* method for you.

Mentioning Your Need for Sponsorship

Including your sponsorship requirement on your covering letter means that you are being *up-front and honest* about your situation and do not want to waste anyone's time. By doing this, you are therefore letting the employer decide for themselves whether they would like to proceed with your application or not.

If you would like to include this information on your cover letter, the best method is to bring it up at the *end of the letter*, so that you at least try to 'win over' the employer with your suitability for the job before they consider your circumstances. You should also include the *contact details* of your *migration agent*, so that the employer can make enquiries if they would like to consider you.

If you do not have a migration agent, you are welcome to use our preferred registered migration agents, whose details you will find in the "*Where to Next*" section of this book.

On the flip side, stating your visa status and requirement for sponsorship on your cover letter will cause, in many cases, a *rejection* of your application before the employer even has an opportunity to view your CV.

Not Mentioning Your Need for Sponsorship

If you were to leave your visa status and requirement for sponsorship *off* your cover letter, and only address your suitability for the job, you will likely *increase* your chance of your application being seriously considered. The reason being: the employer has more chance of '*falling in love*' with your skills and experience only after having *thoroughly reviewed your well-presented Australian CV*; and will then be more *emotionally committed* to you *before* they discover that you require employer sponsorship. If they reject you before viewing your CV – you will miss the chance of this happening.

ACTION POINTS:

1. Follow the steps in this section, and adapt a cover letter accordingly.

2. Visit: www.resumeaustralia.net to view and download effective Australian cover letter templates that come with matching CV templates, or check out the book available here:

   http://www.resumeaustralia.net/resume-cover-letter-ebooks.

Professional Assistance

Many people opt to engage a professional resume writer to create for them an effective resume and cover letter for Australia.

This is a very good option if you **do not trust your own skills** for creating a resume that will really *stand out* and *sell* what you can offer to Australian employers.

Most people don't know the **first place to start** when trying to sell themselves, and it is *much more effective* to have an *objective person* (from the point of view of the *Australian employer*) to analyse your experiences and qualifications and draw attention to the most important aspects on your CV.

When **selecting** a resume writer for the purpose of **applying for jobs in Australia**, I recommend that you select a company who is *skilled* and *experienced* in assisting *overseas nationals* to prepare a resume for the purpose of *employer sponsorship* or your *first job* in Australia.

Resume Australia is a reputable organisation for writing professional, Australian CVs that are strategically developed for employer sponsorship (or your first job) in Australia. Visit: **www.ResumeAustralia.net** for more information, or send an email to: australianjobsearch@gmail.com to make an inquiry about having your CV and cover letter rewritten into an **effective Australian format**.

<u>Do not</u> move on to the next chapter until you have completed your Australian cover letter.

Job Search

"Our goals can only be reached through a vehicle of a plan, in which we must fervently believe, and upon we must vigorously act. There is no other route to success."

- Stephen A. Brennan

Planning Your Job Search

When on a mission to secure employment in Australia, and after creating a competitive Australian CV and a cover letter that meets (or exceeds) the expectations of Australian employers; you then need to **start planning your job search** so that you can be as *effective* as possible and *increase* your success rate.

Without proper planning in your search for jobs in Australia, you will not have a direction to move in, and you may end up going around and around in circles.

You need to ask yourself: "**what is my job search strategy for finding a job in Australia?**"

If your plan is to simply *search for jobs online* and apply, hoping for the best, your job search will likely **end in failure**.

Remember: this is the way **everyone else** is searching for jobs in Australia, and not everyone is successful using this method, especially if they are seeking their **first job** in Australia or if they need **employer sponsorship**.

You therefore **need to be different**, **go the extra mile** and **take the paths** that not all job seekers are *willing*, or *aware*, of treading.

Creating a **powerful** job search strategy, that will assist you to **rise above the rest**, is *essential* to successfully securing a job in Australia.

Where to Start…?

The best place to start is to first decide *exactly* what **type of job** you would ideally like in Australia. Without taking this step, your search will be *blind* and you will not give the impression to Australian employers that you are someone who knows **exactly what they want** and **where they want** to be.

NB – Australian employers (and employers in general) like people who know **exactly what they want**.

This step is also important when finalising your Australian CV and cover letter, so that you can have **targeted marketing documents** for your job search, which in turn will create a more **powerful** job search.

Your Ideal Job

To begin determining what your ideal job in Australia would be, you need to spend some valuable time thinking about *exactly* what your ideal job would look like.

If you're not sure, make a **list** of all the various jobs you have held in the past that you **loved**, followed by a list of all the things that you **liked** most about these jobs, followed by a list of all of the things that you **did not like** about them.

We all have things that we do not like about our work, but the beauty of planning in this way is that you can now decide exactly what you would like your new job to look like, and what you would not like it to include.

For example, you may be an HR Generalist; however, you are finding that what you really love about your work are *projects*, *organisational* and *culture change* and *performance management*. You have also found that what you really don't like is *Payroll* and *highly administrative tasks*. You also like *recruitment*, *attraction* and *retention*; however, you would not like an HR role that was *solely* recruitment orientated.

Now you are starting to paint a good picture of the type of job you should be aiming for in Australia!

ACTION POINT:

Create a list of all of the things you liked about your work (past & present); and a list of all the things that you did not like about your work (past & present).

A table, such as the example below, can help you to organise your answers.

PAST JOBS	LIKES	DISLIKES

Your Ideal Company

Another important aspect of designing the type of job you would *ideally* like, is to think about what *type of company* you would like to work for, for example: a *large, global corporation*; or a *small, family run business*?

A great way to get started on this task is to look at what industry/s you have worked in previously, and making note which of these that you do/did enjoy working in the most.

You should also consider things such as whether you would like to be employed in a *team environment*, in a *specialised field*; or whether you prefer an *autonomous role* with *broad scope*.

Writing down as much detail as possible in this task will really help you to *narrow down* the specifics of the type of company that you would gain the *most satisfaction* from working for.

ACTION POINT:

Write a detailed description of the type of company you would ideally like to work for. Be as descriptive as possible, including things such as type of industry, size of organisation and type of environment.

An example of a way to organise your answers is by creating a table like the one below.

INDUSTRY	SIZE	ENVIRONMENT

Your Ideal Career

Based on your answers to the exercises in the previous two sections, have a think about what **type of job** you would like to be going for in Australia.

Will it be similar to your **current role**? Or would you like to take on a role that has **more responsibility**? Perhaps one of your previous roles turned out to be your **ideal role** and you will now be aiming for that type of role. Have a really good think about this, and write down your answer.

It is also really beneficial to consider what type of role you would like to be working in, in **5 years' time**. You can then keep this in mind when deciding on the **type of company** you would like to work for in Australia.

For example, if you would like the opportunity to move up the 'ranks' in a company, you will need to select a company that has **scope for career progression** so that you would not be limited to the one role indefinitely.

This particular exercise will not only help you to **hone your focus** on jobs that are *ideal* for you and that you will ultimately *excel* in; but will benefit you additionally, by preparing you for these types of questions in any *future interviews*.

ACTION POINTS:

1. Write a detailed description of the type of role you would like to aim for in Australia, now.

2. Write a detailed description of the type of role you would like to see yourself in, in 5 years' time.

3. For both of your above answers, include the responsibilities and duties that you would enjoy, even as far as how many employees you would like to manage or supervise (if this is something you would like to see yourself doing as part of your job). Be as descriptive as possible.

Feel free to create a table similar to that below, to help organise your answers.

IDEAL ROLE	DESCRIPTION
NOW	
IN 5 YEARS	

Adjusting Your CV

Now that you are clear on your ideal job, and therefore the type of jobs you will be aiming for in Australia, it is a good time to go back to your CV and cover letter to adjust these accordingly, so they have a focus around your ideal position.

Are there any *skills* or *experiences* you can add or highlight, in support of the types of jobs you will be aiming for?

Are there perhaps any *courses* you can do to help you to achieve your ideal job? These are all things that you should spend time considering, so as to present yourself as the *ideal candidate* for the types of roles you will be applying for.

Australian Migration and Recruitment Expos

If you haven't already made the move to Australia and need to find a job before you get there, **Careers Fairs and Migration Expos** are a highly effective tool to take advantage of.

These events will offer you the chance to **meet** with Australian employers and representatives who are willing to hire foreign nationals, and who are **actively looking** for skilled candidates who would like to migrate to Australia.

There are regular events held annually, all over the world in this regard, particularly in the UK and Ireland.

Below are some websites with information on up-coming events. You can also try doing a Google search to find other events that are held in your home country.

- Down Under Expo – **www.downunderexpo.com**

- Working In – **www.workingin-australia.com/categories/41**

- Australia Needs Skills – **www.immi.gov.au/skillevents/upcoming-events.htm**

ACTION POINTS:

1. Find out if there are any migration and/or recruitment expos in your area or country.

2. If you find any, make note of the dates, research whether it would be worth-while you attending, and (if yes) make plans to attend

Job Search Websites

In Australia, as with most of the world now, jobs are *more likely* to be advertised on *job search websites*, and *less likely* to be advertised in newspapers.

These days the average person has at least one *computer* at home, has a *smart phone*, or at least has access to the internet through their workplace or internet cafes.

The internet is **fast** and **convenient**. Long gone are the days of going down to the shop to buy the *paper*, trawling through the pages of jobs in the *classifieds* section, writing a cover letter (*by hand*!) and *photocopying* your resume to enclose in an *envelope* then taking it down to the news agency to purchase a *stamp*. You then needed to find a *post office box* to ensure the letter goes in the post before a certain time to make the post that day. Afterwards you would wait for several days, if not weeks, to finally receive a reply in the mail to say that you have not been successful for the job you applied for. Maybe some of you don't remember those days, or they were before your time!

Job search has become so convenient that you can even have suitable jobs sent directly to your inbox and can apply for them with the click of a button. **How times have changed!**

Not only is advertising job vacancies online *convenient*, *fast* and *effective* for employers, but it can also be *a lot* cheaper than advertising in a newspaper, *and* have further reach. Therefore, Australian employers these days tend to advertise their job vacancies through one or more *job search websites*.

The most popular and utilised websites for searching for jobs in Australia are as follows:

- **SEEK – seek.com.au**
  Australia's number 1 job site

- **Career One – careerone.com.au**
  On-line job listings from newspaper advertisements

Other websites you can try:

- **Job Search – jobsearch.gov.au**
  Government run jobs database

- **Jobs Search – jobsearch.com.au**
  Australian job search website

- **My Career – mycareer.com.au**

    Job search and employment opportunities in Australia

- **Jobs – jobs.com.au**

    Australian job search website

- **Jobaroo – jobaroo.com**

    Aimed at the Australian backpacker market

ACTION POINTS:

1. Take some time to browse through the above websites, bookmarking the ones you like best or that have the largest number of jobs that fit your background.

2. Register your details to receive job alerts, upload your CV, and apply for jobs that look suitable.

Recruitment Agencies

Don't let anyone tell you that recruitment agents are your friend! Although perhaps you have figured out this little tip on your own. ☺

For those of you who have seen my YouTube video on the topic (www.youtube.com/watch?v=bldWS-Fcg2k), you will have a better understanding of what I mean.

There is much debate in using recruitment agencies to find employment in Australia, especially when you are applying from your **home country**.

A lot of recruitment agencies in Australia **will not** consider candidates who require sponsorship, or those who have working rights but *not yet in the country*. Simply put, recruitment agents will not go out of their way for foreign nationals to help them find work, as it is harder for the recruiter to "*sell*" the candidate to the employer when the candidate requires *sponsorship* or can't start work *right away* because they're not yet in the country.

Since being a recruitment agent is all about filling positions for their client companies, and filling them fast, recruitment agents prefer to work with local candidates for positions, unless the employer has specified that they are willing to consider overseas nationals.

I therefore do not always recommend using recruitment agencies in Australia if you are applying for jobs from your **home country**, as you will likely find them to be a **big waste of your time**.

Even if you are in Australia and applying for your first job, recruiters won't always be so helpful as they still see you as a '*hard sell*' to the employer because you haven't had any **Australian experience** as yet.

However, if you see some jobs that you really like and decide to go ahead and apply for them through agencies, I have provided you with some tips below so that you **get the most out of recruitment agencies**.

Tip #1 Avoid Recruiters

See if you can find out the name of the **company** the recruitment agency is representing, and then do your own research to get the contact details of the **HR department** or **hiring manager** for that job so you can apply direct to the company and/or hiring manager. **By-passing recruiters is your best chance of being considered for the job.**

Tip #2 Avoid Over-Applying

Do not apply for **several jobs** that are advertised with the **same recruitment agency**. Once you have applied for one job, your resume goes into their *database* and will then be *searchable* so they can consider you for other jobs. Recruiters are generally **not impressed** when a candidate sends through applications for several jobs – particularly when the jobs are *different in nature* – as it can give the impression of **desperateness** – like you would settle for *any job* – something you want to **avoid at all costs**! Recruiters (and employers for that matter) like candidates who are **confident** in the direction they are going in their career, not someone who doesn't really know what job or career path they want to go down. Even if you're not sure, at least *pretend* that you know what you want. ☺

If you do see **more than one job** you would like to apply for with the one recruitment agency, apply for the **most suitable role**, then do a **follow-up call** to the relevant recruiter to advise that there are several roles you would like to be considered for (and have the list with the job codes ready for them). This will also allow you to **develop a relationship** with the agency or consultant and they will *remember* you when your name comes up again.

Tip #3 Use the Telephone

When you see a job that you *really* like and want to apply for, **make a phone call** to the recruiter to find out more about the role and find out whether your skills would *'fit the bill'*. By making **direct contact** with the recruiter you are **establishing a relationship**, and this is also an opportunity for you to find out whether the employer would consider sponsoring an overseas national (if required in your case), as well as enabling you to **sell yourself** a little bit to get some interest.

Tip #4 Follow-Up

Follow-up your application with a telephone call. Again, this helps to **establish and build a relationship**. When a recruiter knows you on a more *personal* level they feel more obliged to *help* you. I can tell you this from *first-hand* experience from being a recruiter – the candidates who phoned the most often were **more likely to get a job** because they were always fresh in your mind, and in a way you just want to *get them off your back*! Even though this is kind of pestering, if you are not the most appropriate person for the job, you are **more likely to be considered** for the role. Be very, *very* careful not to overdo it though, as this method will *backfire*. The *first* follow-up should be **within a week**; then you should not follow up more than **1-2 times per month** after that.

ACTION POINT:

When applying for jobs that are advertised through recruitment agencies, be sure to take the above tips on board, because they will make an immense difference to your job search results!

Sponsored Job Listings

Over the years, I have developed *partnerships* with various Australian *recruitment agencies* to assist them to fill their vacancies. These **recruitment partners** offer positions with **employer sponsorship** in Australia and the jobs are, in some cases, exclusive.

This may sound *backwards* after the previous section stated that recruitment agencies are *unhelpful*; but every now and then, on *very rare occasions*, you do come across recruitment agencies that are helpful, and the key factor is that they are normally associated with **migration agencies**.

You can view the current sponsored jobs list at any time, by visiting: **www.sponsoredjobsinaustralia.com** *and navigating to, "Search Jobs".*

I also advertise all jobs as they become available at the *LinkedIn group*, **Employer Sponsorship Australia (http://linkd.in/1g2eCKP)**.

Sponsored Job Application Procedures

When you visit the sponsored jobs listing via the above link, and have seen a job that you would like to apply for or want to learn more about, click on the job and you will be taken to a page giving more information about the *position on offer*, the **experience** and **skills** required for the job, the **benefits**, **location** and more.

If you feel you fit **all of the criteria** for the job, you can *submit* your interest through the **contact form** at the bottom of the job advert. Be sure to give **full details** of your relevant experience and skills so that it is clear that you **meet the selection criteria**. Those who *meet the criteria* will then be **invited** to send their CV for further consideration.

Due to the number of applications received on a daily basis, if you are **not successful** for the job you have applied for, you will likely **not be contacted**. You are, however, welcome to apply again for any other vacancies that look suitable.

ACTION POINTS:

1. Visit www.sponsoredjobsinaustralia.com and view the job vacancies that are available, submitting your interest only for jobs that you meet the criteria for.

2. Sign up to the mailing list on the "Search Jobs" page, to ensure that you are advised as soon as new jobs are available, so you can apply right away for any suitable vacancies.

NADINE MYERS

The Hidden Job Market

The *downturn in the economy* over previous years has brought about the need for Australian companies to *reassess their budgets* and concentrate on their profit line; which has unfortunately meant having to *lay off* a lot of employees, and *downsize*.

A *reduced number of jobs available* in Australia, and an *increased number of job applicants* in the market (both locally and from overseas) has created a *highly competitive job market* in Australia.

Australian employers have been changing their recruitment methods over the past 10 years or so, and candidates have to adapt to these new methods in order to have success in the Australian job market.

With the cutting back of usage of *recruitment agencies* in many cases, and reducing the costs of *advertising expenses*, Australian employers are no longer relying on *newspapers* for advertising and are even reducing their expenditure on *job boards*, such as **SEEK** (www.seek.com). Instead, some of them are utilising *free job boards*, such as **Gum Tree** (www.gumtree.com.au), using *social networking sites*, such as **LinkedIn** and are also enhancing their own *careers pages* on their company website to attract suitable candidates.

This is what we call the hidden job market: when employers choose <u>not to</u> advertise through the regular channels, and use their <u>own resources</u> and networks.

According to SEEK (**www.seek.com.au**), *Australia's #1 Job Site*, *"many job opportunities are never advertised"*.

It has been estimated that *more than half* of positions vacant in Australia have been filled through the hidden job market, rather than being advertised through the usual channels.

A good example of an organisation that utilises this method of recruiting is Rio Tinto (www.riotinto.com), who do not typically use recruitment agencies and *avoid* using online job boards and newspaper advertising except for the more *specialised roles* that are *harder to fill*. Instead, they have a very *sophisticated careers website* where candidates can apply for jobs, subscribe to a *job mailing list* to receive up-to-date listings on a regular basis – which can mean that subscribers will be the *first to hear* of a suitable vacancy within the organisation. Applications then go into a *pool*, which Rio Tinto can tap into as jobs become available.

This is a very *savvy and innovative* approach to recruiting for companies, and also allows candidates to *pick and choose* who they would like to work for, and *register* their details with those particular organisations. Rio Tinto is definitely not the only company in Australia using this approach, as you will find out when you do your own company research.

Networking is another way to tap into the hidden job market in Australia. Through increasing your Australian networks, contacts and friends, you can find out about jobs *before* they even become available on the market. Don't be afraid to use *social networking* sites to build up your Australian networks, especially *LinkedIn* – every little bit helps!

Using the hidden job market to find employment in Australia is one of the best strategies that you can use; and is where my clients are finding the majority of their successes.

I recommend that you *do your own research* into the hidden job market, and how you can use it; and then ensure that you *tap into* the hidden job market in Australia. If you *do not* make use of this valuable resource, you will effectively be *reducing* the number of opportunities available to you.

If you require assistance with using the hidden job market, I have written entire strategies around using the hidden job market in Australia for job search; and you can learn just how you can use it through the following downloadable guides:

Find Jobs in Oz
(www.findjobsinoz.com) – for those with PR or *working rights* for Australia; or

Find Sponsored Jobs in Australia
(www.sponsoredjobsinaustralia.com) – if you require *Employer Sponsorship*.

Alternatively, there are full online *mentoring programs* that I offer, where I can work with you virtually hand-in-hand to assist you with *every aspect* of your Australian job search, based on your *individual situation*. You can learn more about these *Job Search Mentoring Courses* by visiting: www.NadineMyers.com.

ACTION POINTS:

1. Do your own research into the hidden job market to find out how you can use it to improve your job search results.

2. Ensure you are using your networks and social networking sites to find jobs in Australia, especially LinkedIn.

3. Register your place to have one-on-one mentoring with me (www.nadinemyers.com), to help you put your absolute best foot Forward for your Australian job search; or download one of the guides (from the web links on the previous page) to learn how you can do it yourself.

Planning a Trip to Australia

It is a good idea to plan a trip to Australia if you have not been before, especially if you have been applying for jobs from outside of Australia for some time and are not having any luck.

Planning a trip to Australia will allow you to **explore the country** and work out **where you would like to live**, do some research on the **cost of living**, **buying a house** and a **car**, and generally **setting up your life** there. But more importantly, it will allow you to <u>**attend interviews**</u> with *employers*, *recruiters* and start establishing some *networks* 'on the ground'.

If you can plan a trip to Australia, you should use the time as **effectively as possible** by seeing **as many** employers and recruitment agencies as you can schedule.

Here are some tips on using your trip to Australia to your best advantage:

- **Be prepared**: have all of the *contact numbers* and *addresses* ready of the places you have already applied for jobs, or whom you can apply to once you arrive.

- **Make those all-important follow-up calls** after applying for jobs to *establish the relationship*. Let your contacts know that you will be in their area for a specific length of time only and will be *available to meet*.

- **Be up front** – suggest a couple of *suitable times* that you can meet with them briefly while you are in the area.

- **Drop in to the businesses** that you apply to and ask for the *specific recruiting or hiring manager* who is responsible for the job you have applied for, so you can have a face-to-face chat.

When it is time to head back to your home country, you will at least have **established some relationships**, and have many **contact names and numbers** of people you can follow up with on a regular basis for employment.

NB – Planning a trip for job search can be tricky when applying for tourist visas, and it is best not to mention that this is your purpose for travel as your visa may be rejected due to immigration agents labelling you a 'risk', meaning they will be afraid that you will take up illegal employment in Australia. Obviously you would not plan to do such a thing as it would completely jeopardise your ability to migrate to Australia indefinitely. It is therefore better to state your reason for travel as tourist purposes.

The downloadable guides and online mentoring courses mentioned in the last section all cover the **full details** on how to **plan and prepare** for a trip to

Australia and use the trip to your *absolute advantage*. Go back to the previous section if you would like to learn more about each of these programs.

ACTION POINTS:

1. Set out to plan a trip to Australia as part of your research.

2. Ensure that you set up as many interviews as you can, to make your trip worthwhile.

3. Take caution when applying for a tourist visa, stating your reason for travel as 'tourism purposes'.

Getting Job-Ready

"Success occurs when opportunity meets preparation."

- Zig Ziglar

What Does 'Getting Job-Ready' Mean?

Being job-ready will help to **give you an edge** for securing a job in Australia, and also **speed up the process for migrating**; particularly if you are looking for **employer sponsorship**.

What does this mean exactly?

It means ensuring all the **paperwork** that is required for migrating that can be done in advance is completed; including **skills assessments**, **English language tests** (if required), **police clearance**, **academic transcripts**, **employment references, medical reports** etc.

This also means being **ready to relocate** as soon as a job is secured; so tying up any lose ends with **property**, **selling** things you know you won't take with you, ensuring you don't have a long **notice period** at your work and even **planning** for you or your partner to migrate to Australia ahead of the other to set up, whilst loose ends are tied up back at home (if necessary).

In this Module we will specifically look at the following:

- **English Language Testing**

- **Skills Assessments**

- **Work References**

So let's start with proving your level of English!

English Language Skills

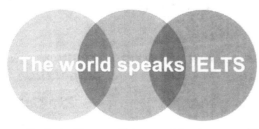

Since Australia is an English speaking country, your **English Language skills** are a very important aspect of your job application. Whether *written* or *spoken*, you will be a **more competitive applicant** if you have **advanced** English language skills, particularly if you will be working in a position which requires *customer liaison* or extensive *communication skills*.

Many migrants to Australia arrive with qualification after qualification; however, their English language skills are **quite poor**. Some migrants choose to study even further, so they can stay in Australia and gain Australian qualifications; however, this doesn't always help them to secure a job, and in fact it can often **make it harder** for them because it often means that they haven't worked in their field for *2-4 years*. Rather than studying a second degree or MBA, I recommend you put your money and time into **improving your English language skills**; because if you can 'talk the talk', then that will do more for you than having more *qualifications*.

Obviously this section only relates to non-English speaking countrymen and women; so if you come from a English speaking country, such as UK, Ireland, Canada, US or other; you can skip to the next course unit.

The issue that many migrants face is that although they are **highly qualified** in their field, due to their **below average English skills**, they are **unable** to gain a position in their field and quite often will have to settle for a role within a completely different field, such as hospitality. I have seen this a lot in Australia, and it saddens me greatly to see such qualified people who are clearly good at what they do, have their skills and talent wasted in a job that does not use those skills and qualifications.

For those with PR, you will already have passed the English requirement to get your visa.

For those who are looking for **employer sponsorship**, you **need to have IELTS** or equivalent, **before** you can migrate to Australia.

Many people make the mistake of not getting this sorted **before they apply** for jobs in Australia. From my experience, given the time it already takes for a visa to be processed, employers **don't want to have to wait** an extra month or two for you to sit your IELTS exam. They therefore **expect** you to already have this done if you are **serious** about migrating to Australia. If you haven't, then they may doubt whether you are serious, or indeed whether you have the required English skills to meet the Australian immigration requirements.

Do your research. At the time of creating this course, you needed to have at minimum an overall IELTS test score of *5.0*, AND a minimum score of 4.5 *in each section* of the four sections (*reading, writing, speaking, listening*). You can learn more about the English requirements for migrating to Australia at: www.border.gov.au.

To find out where you nearest IELTS testing centre is, go to: **www.ielts.org**; and make sure you prioritise booking your exam, ahead of applying for jobs. If you are not confident that you will pass this exam, before you waste your money on sitting the exam, I recommend that you do an English refresher course before booking your IELTS exam, to ensure you are aiming for the highest scores that you can. Even though the minimum requirements, as stated above, are quite low; you will have a better chance of being employed if your scores are as high as you can manage.

Visit the Australian immigration website to find out what the minimum score that you require *for your profession* is, so you can aim for that score or *higher*.

Remember, even though the above scores are the minimum scores that you need to migrate to Australia (in most professions); you will increase your likelihood of being hired if you can achieve as high a score as possible.

You can learn more on IELTS, by watching the below short video clip:

https://youtu.be/p1UeGt-OtWE

ACTION POINTS:

1. If your native language is not English, go to the Australian immigration site (www.border.gov.au) and find out what minimum IELTS scores you require for your profession, in order to qualify for migrating to Australia.

2. If you are not confident that you will achieve the required IELTS score, or would like to aim for the highest score that you can (recommended), book to do an English refresher course to improve your level of English *before* you sit the exam.

3. Go to: www.ielts.org (International English Language Testing System) to find out where your nearest testing centre is, and to book to sit your IELTS exam asap.

4. If your IELTS scores are not sufficient for migrating to Australia, do Further study so you can improve them and sit the test again until you achieve the desired scores.

Skills Assessment

In many cases, particularly if you are from a **non-English speaking country**, you will need to complete a **skills assessment** before you can migrate to Australia.

If you have PR, you would already have completed this process.

However, if you are only starting the process of applying for PR, or if you require employer sponsorship, this is something you will need to look into **before** you can submit an application for a visa.

The purpose of the skills assessment is to ensure that your level of education **meets the Australian standard**.

Skills assessments **can take some time**; for example, the **VETASSESS** assessment (www.vetassess.com.au) takes between **4-12 weeks**, and **sometimes longer**, depending on where the applicant is **from**, and the **complexity** of the case. It is therefore a very good idea to **organise** your skills assessment in **advance**, if it is required in your case.

If you're not sure whether you require a skills assessment, you can find out by following these steps:

1. Go to the SOL or CSOL, where you found the **occupation** that you investigated whether you qualify for.

2. On the particular skills list, next to the name of the occupation, you will find two other columns: **ANZSCO Code**, and **Assessing Authority**.

3. It is the **Assessing Authority** you need, and in this column you will find the name of the relevant assessing authority for you (e.g. VETASSESS). Simply **click** on the name of the assessing authority and you will be taken to the **website** for that assessing authority.

4. You can now investigate whether it is a requirement for you to complete a skills assessment or not. If you're not sure, **contact** the assessing authority direct to find out.

Once you have your positive skills assessment at hand, you will be in a ***much stronger position*** for applying for *sponsored jobs* in Australia; as employers will be more likely to consider sponsoring you if this step of the process is already complete.

If you are applying for PR, you will be that one step closer in the application process as well.

ACTION POINTS:

1. Find out whether you require a skills assessment to migrate to Australia, by following the steps on the previous page.

2. If required, locate your relevant assessing authority, and start the process of obtaining your skills assessment as soon as possible.

Employment References

It is best that you get organised and arrange to have **written employment references** from past employers as soon as you can.

The importance of having these references is not only for the purpose of your migration application; but also in case Australian employers request these from you when applying for jobs.

When deciding on **which employers** to obtain references from, it is best to select those where your **most relevant experience** was gained (for the occupation you qualify for), and to choose the **specific referee** who will give the *most glowing* reference for you.

The referee you choose must also be someone whom you reported to.

Once you have selected **who to ask** for a written reference, and you should ask **as many as possible**; you should ensure that they give as much information on their written reference as they can, including:

- As much detail as possible on the **responsibilities** in your role

- **Dates** of your employment with the company (make sure these correspond with your CV!)

- **Status of employment** (i.e. whether you were part time, casual, full time or a temp or contract employee)

- Some indication of your **performance** in that role

The reference, where possible, should be written on **company letter head**, and should also include the **contact details** of the person, both *phone* and *email*, so that they can be contacted if further information is required.

It may be that you *already* have some references of this nature at hand, after completing the skills assessment process in the previous course unit. If that is the case, you should be pleased that this step is already complete!

ACTION POINTS:

1. Make a list of your previous jobs that are relevant to the occupation you qualify for, for migration to Australia.

2. Select the most appropriate person/s to ask to write a reference for you, based on the points on the previous page.

3. Give your referees guidelines of what the written reference needs to say, and even prepare a draft to make this task easier for them and to encourage their speedy response.

4. Aim to obtain as many written references as you can.

Checklists

"Most people have the will to win, few have the will to prepare to win."

- Bobby Knight

Below you will find two checklists to help you stay organised with your migration planning:

- One for those who are seeking employer sponsorship; and

- One for PR or other work visa holders

Please note that these checklists are a *simple guide*, highlighting the key steps in your job search and migration planning; and do not cover every single step that you need to complete.

Checklist for Employer Sponsorship Job Seekers

1 Find Out if You Qualify	▪ Own Research ▪ Migration Assessment
2 Prepare Marketing Materials	▪ Australian Resume/CV ▪ Cover Letter ▪ LinkedIn
3 Plan Job Search	▪ Ideal Job & Job Search Strategy ▪ Migration Expos ▪ Recruitment Agencies & Job Search Websites ▪ Hidden Job Market
4 Get Job-Ready	▪ IELTS ▪ Skills Assessment ▪ Employment References ▪ Other Documents
5 Plan a Trip to Australia	▪ Set Aside Dates ▪ Plan Your Locations ▪ Set Goals ▪ Book Interviews
6 Prepare to Attend Interviews in Australia	▪ Set Aside Cost of Flights ▪ Speak to Employer About Short Notice Required
7 Prepare to Move	▪ Give Notice at Work ▪ Sell House, Business etc. ▪ Sort Out Shipping of Furniture, Pets etc.
8 Set Yourself up in Australia	▪ Housing ▪ Vehicle ▪ Banking ▪ Schooling (if required)

Checklist for PR Holders

1 Prepare Marketing Materials	▪ Australian Resume/CV ▪ Cover Letter ▪ LinkedIn
2 Plan Job Search	▪ Ideal Job & Job Search Strategy ▪ Migration Expos ▪ Recruitment Agencies & Job Search Websites ▪ Hidden Job Market
3 Plan a Trip to Australia	▪ Set Aside Dates ▪ Plan Your Locations ▪ Set Goals ▪ Book Interviews
4 Set a Deadline to Migrate	▪ Plan to Migrate by a Set Date ▪ Book Flexible Flights
5 Prepare to Move	▪ Give Notice at Work ▪ Sell House, Business etc. ▪ Sort Out Shipping of Furniture, Pets etc.
6 Set Yourself up in Australia	▪ Housing ▪ Vehicle ▪ Banking ▪ Schooling (if required)

Success Stories

"Smart people learn from their own mistakes.
Smarter people learn from other people's mistakes.
The smartest people learn from other people's
successes."

- Unknown

The Benefit of Success Stories

I decided it would be beneficial to include some detailed success stories as part of this book, so that you have some real-life examples of people who have used some of the job search strategies that I teach to find jobs in Australia – and did so with fruitful results!

These stories should both inspire you, and give you additional guidance on how to find a job in Australia.

Please find in the following section, four comprehensive case studies of people who aimed their target towards finding a sponsored job in Australia, and scored!

Although these are employer sponsorship success stories, they will still benefit PR holders, as the methods used here can be duplicated for your job search, no matter what your situation.

Read these stories, and learn from the techniques and strategies that these successful job hunters used, so that you can increase your chance of success. If they can do it, so can you!

Landscape Gardener Finds Sponsorship in Perth

Richard Pease, a senior landscaper from the UK, found sponsorship in Perth, Western Australia.

At 40 years of age, Richard had initially made an application for a GSM visa based on his skills as a Landscape Gardener. However, soon after, the DIAC made announcements that they were temporarily postponing the processing of many visas, including Richard's, which forced him to take a different approach.

"I could not wait until the projected processing date (four years later), so Nadine Myers was recommended to me by a migration agent," Richard said; and he commenced his search for sponsored employment shortly after.

Richard had been applying for jobs from outside of Australia, and hence his decision to engage an Emigration Job Search Strategist to assist him with his search.

Richard also took a very proactive approach with his job sponsorship search and left no stone unturned until he received an offer of sponsorship that he was happy with.

Being proactive in his job search, Richard sought out landscaping companies in Australia and applied to them directly.

"I simply went onto [the] Australian Yellow Pages website and sent my CV accompanied by cover letter to at least 150 Landscaping Companies," said Richard.

Although he did most of the 'legwork' himself, Richard says:

"Much of the credit goes to Nadine and her Sponsored Jobs in Australia mentoring, as without that all-important re-vamped/re-formatted CV together with help on [the] cover letter, I would definitely not have been as appealing to any prospective employer."

From the time that Richard engaged my assistance and job sponsorship search strategies to assist him with his job sponsorship search, to the time that he had a signed contract from his sponsor, was approximately 6 months.

The assistance I provided, together with the many companies Richard contacted directly; brought about many interviews and Richard in the end received four job offers in the regions of Adelaide, Canberra and Perth. Having the option of four jobs, Richard was able to make a decision based not only on the role itself, but also on the location and lifestyle which he wanted for himself and his family.

Richard therefore selected the role in Perth, and received a 457 Temporary Business Visa, valid for four years. This visa had restrictions upon it so that he could not work in NSW, QLD or VIC.

Richard's Top Tips

- "Get advice on securing the best exchange rate for your money"

- "I would recommend making a visit to see where in Australia you would like to settle". Richard and his family moved to Perth, however, he admits that he would have preferred to have waited for a job placement/sponsor in Melbourne or Sydney.

- "As to advice I would have to offer others, I would definitely recommend any person seeking sponsorship/jobs to get in touch with Nadine from nadinemyers.com."

- "Nadine's package offers a brilliant job search strategy which I also made use of"

Richard feels that the main things that helped him to find sponsored employment in Australia were:

"Being bold and getting my name out there. I sold myself, I did not give up and eventually I managed to get four job offers via telephone interviews."

In Hindsight

The most challenging part of finding a job in Australia for Richard was the "endless paperwork I had to produce when acquiring my skills assessment by TRA (Trades Recognition of Australia)."

Richard also feels that he made the mistake of emigrating to Perth with his family without making a visit first. At the time, Richard thought that the money spent on this expensive holiday would be better spent towards the cost of moving. "But in hindsight, it would have been money well spent," he says.

Richard found the migration process 'difficult'. "It would have been much easier had the DIAC not done a U-turn on the processing of my visa to start with," he says.

Richard had appointed a UK based migration agent, but decided against using the agent in the end as he felt that they were 'dragging their heels slightly and were not proactive enough.' He did end up losing his deposit due to this; however, he was not sorry about that decision.

On Life in Australia

Richard did not find 'any challenges whatsoever regarding fitting in with his work colleagues'. However, he did report that he had heard from other migrants, particularly those in the health and medical sector, that they had issues settling in because they had been placed at the bottom of the ladder, as well as being slightly left out by colleagues. In Richard's experience, he feels that this scenario does not apply to the trades industry.

In Richard's opinion, the best thing about migrating to Australia is the 'weather, lifestyle, and laid-back approach'.

"The Australians are a very nice approachable nation of people. I/we also feel very safe here, much more so than in UK", said Richard.

Richard's Job Search Strategy and Advice in Brief:

- Have a professional create a high-impact CV for the Australian job market

- Receive advice and guidance from an Australian Emigration Job Search Strategist

- Implement a tailored job search strategy developed by a specialist, such as www.nadinemyers.com

- Be proactive in your search and seek out companies you can approach directly – Richard used www.YellowPages.com.au to get names and contact details of suitable companies

- Apply directly to at least 150 companies, and follow up on your job applications with a friendly email or phone call

- Arrange several interviews so that you can have a choice of location

- If you are not sure about the location of your job offer, make a trip to Australia to explore the area and determine whether you would be happy living there

Richard's Final Recommendations:

"The professionalism, experience and advice that came with this specialist package were second to none and I would recommend any person seeking employment in Australia get in touch with Nadine as a first-stop shop!"

RESOURCE BOX

www.SponsoredJobsInAustralia.com, www.FindJobsInoz.com & www.NadineMyers.com – you can engage Australia's Emigration Job Search Strategist as part of your job sponsorship search to assist you with creating a high-impact and competitive Australian CV and Cover Letter, as well as a tailored Australian Job Search Strategy for you to implement.

Yellow Pages – a business directory for finding details of companies in your industry whom you can apply to direct. To start your research now, visit: www.yellowpages.com.au.

Chef Finds Sponsorship in Newcastle

Paul Wilson, a highly experienced Catering Manager and Head Chef from the UK, found job sponsorship in Australia after a reasonably short period applying for jobs from outside of Australia.

Paul and his wife, Marcy, were granted a 457 sponsorship visa and migrated to Newcastle, north of Sydney, just in time to enjoy their first Christmas in Australia.

Paul had a couple of advantages going towards him in his search for employer sponsorship:

- He exudes an addictive positivity in his attitude

- He has an optimistic outlook on life

- He was confident that he would find sponsorship in Australia

- He was determined to succeed, and to do all that he could to make is dream a reality

At 40 years of age, Paul had many years' experience behind him working as a chef and catering manager in the Navy, and branching out in the last few years with his own commendable business ventures, including converting a boat into a successful floating restaurant in the UK.

Paul found his job search reasonably easy, engaging my one-on-one assistance, and using www.seek.com.au and search engines to find jobs that matched what he was looking for.

Paul had been searching for jobs in Australia for about 6 weeks when he was offered his current role, after participating in a telephonic interview process.

Paul's advice to people who are applying for sponsored jobs from overseas, is to 'never give up, and if you aren't that fussy about where you go in Australia it is easier'. This is good advice, especially the part about never giving up, because in most cases when people fail it is because they decide to no longer try. Being open to locations in Australia will also go in your favour because in many cases jobs are available in regional areas, and most people want to be located in or near a major city. In Paul's case, he was happy to go for a smaller city or town.

When asked what he found to be the most challenging thing about finding a job in Australia, Paul answered, "Nothing"; and advised that he found the migration process 'totally painless'. Paul's entire job search was very smooth and efficient, he received positive interest in his skills and experience and was offered a position after just two telephone interviews; migrating to Newcastle, Australia (NSW) without a hitch.

Paul and Marcy actually came out to Australia on a visitor's visa after receiving their job offer and whilst their 457 visa was in process, so that they could arrange housing and settle into their new life prior to starting work in Australia. Paul and Marcy enjoy living an extraordinary life, and for that reason, were on the lookout for a houseboat to set up house in!

Paul used a migration agent that was selected by the sponsoring company, and found the experience 'painless', as they 'had all required documents to hand including full police reports, CVs, references for the last 3 years, marriage certificates etc.'

It is therefore a good idea to do your own research and start gathering all the required documents before applying for 457 sponsorship, as it will tremendously speed up the process when you find a sponsor.

Chefs are on the list of occupations in demand in many of Australia's States and Territories; and since there are more than 7350 restaurants listed on the de Groots Best Restaurants of Australia list (http://www.bestrestaurants.com.au/), and many more cafes, pubs, hotel restaurants and other restaurants in all regions of Australia – it is no wonder that chefs are having an easy time finding sponsored positions in Australia.

At the time of Paul's sponsorship, I had been involved in more than four chef sponsorship cases in a three month period, and all cases found employer sponsorship in regions of their preferences, after having their CV professionally prepared to Australian competitive standards, and engaging the Sponsored Jobs in Australia package (www.sponsoredjobsinaustralia.com) to assist them to seek out and apply for sponsored positions. One particular chef was a new graduate from a chef school in South Africa; however, the majority of chefs who have found success have had a significant amount of experience behind them (at least 10 years) and/or a specialty cuisine such as Asian cuisine. We have found that employers are most interested in UK, European and Filipino chefs when it comes to sponsorship; unless the chef has a speciality cuisine that will benefit their establishment.

Nationalities I have worked with include UK, South African, Malaysian, Dutch, Italian and Singaporean; and locations that my clients have found sponsorship have included regional NSW, Melbourne & regional VIC, regional QLD, and regional WA. I have found Western Australia in general, to be very open to sponsoring chefs as well as other professionals; although all regions of Australia seem to be opening up to sponsoring overseas nationals. The sponsored positions that our clients secured were based in club, restaurant, pub, bakery and hotel environments.

A Final Note from Paul:

"To have the support of professionals is a must in the search for sponsored jobs and obviously the old saying, 'if you at first don't succeed, try, try again' is paramount. I was lucky as the process took about 6 weeks and my wife and I fly to Sydney just before Xmas which is nice.My words of wisdom are: search yourself as well as using professional assistance, and never give up."

Paul also advises that you should keep a track record of which jobs you are applying for so that when you start receiving phone calls, you can refer to this list and know which job the call relates to. This way you will make a better impression on the interviewer. The Job Search Tracker included in the Sponsored Jobs in Australia Package is recommended for this purpose. I also recommend following up on each application you make, within 5 days of applying and tracking your progress in your Job Search Tracker.

In Summary, Paul's Strategy for Finding Employer Sponsorship in Australia Was:

- Have an effective Australian resume prepared before you start applying for jobs, such as those included in this package, or through ResumeAustralia.net

- Engage the support of professionals, such as the Sponsored Jobs in Australia package, as part of your job search (www.sponsoredjobsinaustralia.com or www.findjobsinoz.com)

- Search for jobs using job search engines and job search websites such as seek.com.au

- Be open to all areas of Australia to increase your chance of finding a sponsor

- Gather all your required documents for your sponsorship application in advance to speed up the application process

- Keep track of all job applications you make so you can respond quickly to any telephone interviews

- Remain positive and focused

- Never give up

- "If at first you don't succeed, try, try again"

Toolmaker Finds Sponsorship in Brisbane

Tanja and Will, a young couple of 24 and 25 years of age from Germany, fell in love with Australia when they came on a Working Holiday Visa a few years ago. It was then that they decided that Australia was where they wanted to live.

Tanja is a Pharmacy Technician with five years' experience in Compounding and Dispensing (in Germany), with also an apprenticeship as a Beauty Therapist. Will is a qualified Toolmaker, and originally applied for the 175 Skilled Permanent Visa; however, his occupation was removed from the Skilled Occupation List shortly after, meaning that their 175 visa application could take up to two years to process.

They started to explore their alternate options, and realised that employer sponsorship may be their only option if they want to migrate sooner. They therefore commenced the process of applying for jobs from Germany, although they found it very difficult as they did not receive any responses, so had no idea what they were doing wrong or how to improve their results.

When their frustration peaked, they made the brave decision to enter Australia on a 6 month Visitor's Visa, as they felt they could make more of an impact and make more positive progress on their job search if they were in Australia when applying for jobs.

The couple arrived on the Gold Coast in Queensland, Australia, and were both trying separately to find sponsorship, as they knew that if one found sponsorship, the other could remain in Australia and work too. Four months later, their hard work paid off, and Will found an employer who was willing to sponsor him as a Toolmaker! Their application was submitted, and the visa granted just 6 weeks later, allowing them both to celebrate and settle into their new life in Queensland.

It was a 457 visa that Will was sponsored on, allowing him to be employed as a Toolmaker for the one employer for the period of the visa; and since Will and Tanja are a defacto couple, Tanja was also granted the rights to live and work in Australia for the same period of time; although Tanja's visa allows for her to work for whomever she pleases during the length of the visa. At the completion of their 457 visa, Will can then ask the company to sponsor their permanent residency application, or look at their other visa options.

It was not until they returned to Australia that they were able to make more of an impact on their job search, due to the power of being able to meet with people face-to-face; meaning that people were more receptive to them, compared to when they were applying for jobs from Germany.

Since the couple had already applied for the 175 Skilled Permanent Visa, they already had their IELTS test scores, had arranged for their references and certificates to be translated into English, and they also obtained a positive skills assessment for Will as Tookmaker; they were in a "job-ready" position, and had the confidence to come back to Australia on a serious job search.

Although it took four months to find sponsorship in Australia, they found that there were several companies who were interested in them both, however, these companies were unable or unwilling to sponsor them. Those particular opportunities did not work out in their favour; however the fact that they received positive interest from companies was enough to spur them on and just keep trying. It was certainly worth the effort; and a day of celebration when they finally managed to find a sponsor for Will.

One of the tips that Tanja and Will offer to others who are seeking job sponsorship in Australia is to, "*improve your CV by using the www.resumeaustralia.net site*". They found that after improving their CVs so that they were more effective for Australia, they received more positive responses from their job search.

The Job Search Strategy That Tanja and Will Followed and That They Recommend for Other Job Seekers is as Follows:

> "*Ask a lot of people where they are working and drive there directly. Or just look [up] the addresses on www.yellowpages.com.au. Drive there and give them your CV. If you send them an online application, call them a few hours later and ask them if they have received it. To get into the hidden job market instead of applying for open positions. Don't mention that you are looking for sponsorship and write an (Australian) address on the CV. If they reply you can tell them otherwise they delete it straight away even if you are a good person.*"

When asked what the main thing was that helped them to find a sponsored job in Australia, they answered "*talking to people*". This was made much easier once they were in Australia, and they also then had the opportunity to make face-to-face visits to employers.

What Tanja and Will found to be the most challenging part of their job search was to "*tell the employer that [they] need a sponsorship visa*". Although they had a lot of people interested in them both, they found that announcing the truth of their situation often created a brick wall. However, by not mentioning this fact up front, they were able to meet with many employers and this gave them confidence that their skills were marketable and it was just a matter of time and patience.

Tanja and Will do not regret their decision to go to Australia to search for employment, and would not change a thing about their job search if they had to do it all over again. They were very grateful to have enough money to support themselves during the process and if you are planning on doing something similar, I recommend that you have enough money to cover your expenses for at least 6 months (including a return ticket to your home country).

Once the pair received their visas, Tanja was able to secure employment too, and did so easily from all of the contacts that she had already made over the four month period. When asked what the biggest challenge about integrating into the Australian culture and lifestyle was, they answered that the language had been the toughest thing, since German is their first language.

Both Tanja and Will have found that Australia is meeting the expectations they had of the country before migrating, and in fact are finding the conditions and lifestyle better than what they had in Germany. "*I need to work less [hours] than in Germany and get better money. I live close to the ocean and have an easy going life*", says Tanja, content with her new life in Australia.

The migration process they both found quite difficult due to the constant changes to the rules. "*You always need to be up to date to make sure you can still apply for migration*", said Tanja.

The 457 employer sponsorship visa was applied for onshore, and a migration agent that was based in Queensland, Australia, was engaged for the sponsorship application. Tanja and Will found the experience of using a migration agent very good. "*He prepared all the paper and was answering all my questions*," said Tanja. The agent that they used was selected by the sponsoring employer.

Tanja and Will find that the best thing about migrating to Australia is "*the weather and the multicultural people in Australia*". However, the one "let-down" that they had experienced was that Australia doesn't "*have the same food in the shops like in Europe.*"

Tanja and Will had the advantage of knowing so much already about Australia, since they had already spent one year there on their Working Holiday Visa, and they knew that they wanted to live in Queensland. They had learned all that they could about applying for employer sponsorship through their research, and also through learning from their own experience when applying for sponsored jobs.

In Summary, Tanja and Will's Strategy for Finding Employer Sponsorship in Australia Was:

- Go out to Australia as part of your job search

- Stay on top of the migration rules and laws

- Be prepared and organised, ensuring you have all of the necessary documents you need to apply for sponsorship

- Ensure you have sufficient funds to support yourself without work in Australia for at least 6 months

- Have an effective Australian resume prepared before you start applying for jobs

- Talk to people – after every application, follow up with a phone call

- Make personal visits with your CV to companies where you can

- Use the hidden job market, and don't just apply for jobs through job search websites

- Search for potential employers using www.yellowpages.com.au

- Don't mention that you are looking for employer sponsorship until the interview

- Remove your home address from your CV and include an Australian address and contact number

- Choose an area of Australia that you know you would love to live and spend all your time and energy applying for jobs and staying focused

Information Security Professional Receives Multiple Offers in 2 Weeks

Michael Carthy, an IT / Information Security Professional from the UK, reached out recently to share the amazing success he has had following the purchase and implementation of the Sponsored Jobs in Australia ePackage (www.sponsoredjobsinaustralia.com).

Mike followed the instructions for creating an attractive, Australian CV and deciding to focus his job search efforts on LinkedIn; adapting the strategy, injecting some of his personality into his approach to potential employers, and achieving incredible results – received multiple offers of sponsorship in just TWO WEEKS using his chosen strategy.

Michael has generously given me permission to share this strategy widely so that many people can benefit from it.

Using this strategy, Mike says, "*I received some interesting responses, mostly positive, but also several assuring me that what I was aiming for was almost impossible. It proves that sometimes you just need to be persistent and ignore the naysayers.*"

Very good advice! And because he did not take the negative responses to heart, he was able to stay strong with his strategy and the results were really astounding.

Mike says, "*LinkedIn is vastly underrated and (I suspect) highly underutilised by people searching for sponsors.*"

I cannot agree more with him, and seeing the results that participants are having on my job search mentoring courses (www.nadinemyers.com), is just confirmation of this.

The hard stats from Mike's strategy are as follows:

- Approximately 100 people were contacted over a period of two weeks

- From those, Mike received *three* Skype interviews, *two* formal offers and *one* acceptance!

100 really does seem to be the magic number to hit to receive a positive response, and I have seen this in my own experience over the years. What is even more important though, is to ensure that they are key people that you are approaching; i.e. the *decision makers* when it comes to hiring for the company in your occupation.

Mike is confident that his strategy will work for most people, 'as long as they are driven enough'.

Mike's LinkedIn strategy is as follows:

- Create a LinkedIn account. Build your profile as thoroughly as possible.

- Have your **resume professionally edited**. Make sure it also tallies up with the information on LinkedIn.

- Identify your **dream role**. What industry, companies, people, locations etc. do you want to work in /with?

- Identify the **people who have the power** (authority, contacts, influence etc.) to get you a job in the industries / places that interest you.

- **LinkedIn advanced search** is your No. #1 friend (obtain a 30 day free trial). For example, one of my searches would have been something like the following: INDUSTRY: IT; TITLE: Recruiter OR Manager; LOCATION: Brisbane; EXPERIENCE: Senior Manager / Partner / Director / Owner (i.e. the decision makers). You can even specify COMPANY SIZE (do you want to work for a Fortune 500 or an SME?).

- At this point you should have a **list of influential decision makers** that work in the place you'd like to live, in an industry that you want to work in. And guess what? They've got the authority to hire you directly. It's time to begin making some connections.

- **Connect** with the relevant people from those results. I personally connected with EVERY SINGLE PERSON LinkedIn returned. This is risky however – since LinkedIn can ban you temporarily if too many people decline your invitation with "I don't know this person". Profile picture (in my opinion) is key here – ENSURE YOU'RE SMILING. People want to connect with happy, approachable people.

- Once you've got acceptance notifications rolling in you're making great progress. At this stage you'll be able to **message these decision makers directly**. Compose a very carefully worded message and hit send. At this point there's nothing else that you can do other than sit back and wait.

Here is an example of the message Mike sent to his new 'decision maker' LinkedIn contacts:

Subject: Is it you?

Message:

Hello!

Thank you for accepting my connection. You're probably wondering why somebody from the UK has decided to connect with you – and for good reason. I'm currently seeking to expand my professional network in the hope that somebody out there can put me in touch with my future employer.

I'm an experienced network systems engineer with more than 5 years infrastructure experience gained within a managed services environment; using technologies such as Windows Server, Virtualization, networking, security, Cloud services and VOIP.

I'm now looking to jump across the pond permanently, and in doing so find a business that can offer me the professional growth opportunities and long term commitment that I need to really take my career to the next level.

With a natural flair for dealing with customers, fantastic communication skills and a passion for dealing with people, I'm hoping that by sharing this with you there's a small chance that either you or somebody you know may be able to assist me with the most important move of my career.

I'm ideally looking for sponsorship opportunities in the Brisbane and Sydney areas with creative, forward thinking employers that have a passion for delivering great service.

If you believe that you might be able to assist me then please do drop me a message – every conversation, connection, referral, pointer, recommendation and suggestion is absolutely invaluable.

I'd like to thank you for taking the time to read, and wish every success with your own professional journey.

Best wishes,

Mike

As you can see, Mike has shown a bit of his ***personality*** in his approach, as well as come across as very friendly and conversational, grateful for any assistance, and as having a regard for the contact person's own success. ***This is very powerful***.

I recommend that if you are going to try this approach out for yourself, that you word your messages in your own conversational style, so that you can display a bit of *your own* personality.

It is very important to be friendly in your approach, non-demanding, interested in them and show gratitude for any assistance they can offer.

Mikes' plans changed recently, meaning he has had to postpone his move to Australia, which meant ***turning down*** the offers that were on the table for him. However, Mike is very confident that he won't have an issue finding sponsorship again by applying his strategy when he is in a position again to make the move.

More Success Stories

If you really enjoyed reading these success stories, you will love all the others that share just as much detail and useful tips and strategies that you can implement.

The full range of success stories are included in the extended guides for finding jobs in Australia:

www.findjobsinoz.com

www.sponsoredjobsinaustralia.com

They are also included as part of the 8-week job search mentoring course, which you can learn more about by visiting: **www.NadineMyers.com**.

If you would like to read testimonials on the 8-week course, you can read the most recent ones on the website (www.nadinemyers.com).

Final Word

"Through perseverance many people win success out of what seemed destined to be certain failure."

- Benjamin Disraeli

Finding a job in Australia, especially an employer sponsored job, is no easy feat.

Yes, you do hear of those circumstances where someone applies for a job in Australia, has a telephone or Skype interview, and then is employed by the Australian company and living in Australia within a few short months.

However, these situations are rare, unless you have skills that are extremely high in demand, or you approach the right employer at the right time. In the majority of cases, finding employment in Australia can take a lot longer – even up to 6 months plus.

Whatever situation you find yourself in, this book will guide you on how to get started with a more pro-active and targeted job search; and to learn more and take your job search to the next level, there are more detailed guides available covering *ALL* of the strategies that have enabled others to secure employer sponsorship in Australia, or helped them to secure employment faster if they had Permanent Residency or a Working Holiday Visa.

The strategies set out in the *more advanced* courses, ePackages and books available *have worked for others.* This means that by applying these strategies yourself, you will dramatically increase *your* likelihood of securing a suitable position in Australia.

However, for legal reasons, I cannot guarantee that you will find success by applying all, or any, of the strategies in the courses or books available. After all, I cannot control the demands of the Australian job market (unfortunately!) and I also can't control just how diligently and consistently you will be in applying each of the relevant strategies to your job search – not to mention how you would perform in interviews. All of these things are out of my control.

However, the most diligent participants of my courses and readers of my books have seen a dramatic increase in their success rate, including interviews and even job offers – where previously they were receiving no response from their job applications.

I would like to take this opportunity to remind you that one of the main qualities **common to all people who secure jobs in Australia** is that *their dream was strong enough* that they *remained focused and persistent* until they reached their goal.

If you believe the saying, "*where there is a will, there is a way*", and you are determined to work towards your goal of finding a job in Australia until you reach it; then you are likely to be one of the many who migrate to Australia with a job.

I hope you have found some value in this course and that it has helped you onto the right path for finding a job in Australia.

If/once you do find a job in Australia; I would love to hear your story. Please contact us at **australianjobsearch@gmail.com**.

The next section will help to direct you on *Where to Next*.

Where to Next

"If you really want to do something, you will find a way. If you don't, you will find an excuse."

- Jim Rohn

Further Reading & Assistance

If you have found this course to be a good introduction to getting started in your job search, but you would like some more in-depth information, more one-on-one guidance, more step-by-step strategies and more overall assistance with your job search, there are various options to help you reach your job search goals set out below.

Books & Further Reading

This current book you have just completed, reached #1 in the Amazon top 100 best sellers of its category on Kindle in the first month it was released; and is also available as a free online course at: www.nadinemyers.com (*"Australian Job Search: How to Get Started"*).

Other books available on Amazon are my resume and cover letter writing guides for Australia, including one for employer sponsorship.

All books currently available on Amazon include:

- *Find a Job in Australia*

- *CVs for Job Sponsorship in Australia*

- *Australian Resumes: Steps to Creating an Effective Australian Resume*

- *Australian Cover Letters: Steps to Creating an Effective Australian Cover Letter*

You can access all of my available books here:
http://www.amazon.com/Nadine-Myers/e/B00LA4U73K

Do-It-Yourself Australian Job Search

I have created some DIY type packages for people who are quite independent, confident in their ability to follow instructions, are advanced MS Word users and do not currently have the budget to engage a job search strategist to assist them in their job search. If that sounds like you – read on!

There are two separate downloadable packages: the first is for PR Holders and the second is for those seeking employer sponsorship. Follow the links below for further information on these packages, and details on how to purchase.

Find Sponsored Jobs in Australia ePackage:
www.sponsoredjobsinaustralia.com

Find Jobs in Oz: www.findjobsinoz.com

One-on-One Job Search Assistance

These are 8-week mentoring courses that are suitable for *serious job seekers only*. I say this because only the people who fully dedicate themselves to this 8-week course are likely to have success in securing a position, and since I can only take on a handful of people every month for this course, I only like to deal with people who are serious and committed to finding a job in Australia.

I have had amazing feedback on these courses from people who were having no response in their job search, to all of a sudden receiving invitations for interviews, and even job offers (including sponsorship). You can view some testimonials here: http://nadinemyers.com/testimonials/.

There are two separate courses at present: one for employer sponsorship seekers, and one for PR holders who are seeking their first job. Both courses benefit you with my guidance and recommendations for your particular situation; and include on-going support through the Employer Sponsorship Mentoring group on LinkedIn. These courses are more in-depth than the introductory course based on this book, and include videos, job search tools, downloads and tasks to submit for assessment so you can receive feedback on your progress.

For full details of each course, please visit: http://nadinemyers.com/courses/

To read testimonials from past participants of the above courses, please visit: http://nadinemyers.com/testimonials/.

Professional Australian Resume & Cover Letter Assistance

I have been assessing resumes for Australia since 2000; and have been writing tailored resumes for overseas job seekers migrating to Australia since 2008. The satisfaction rate I receive from my resumes is 100%, and feedback from clients has included the sharing wonderful success stories of interviews and job offers. I know the difference my services make to my clients, and therefore take on each new client with enthusiasm!

To view the resume and cover letter writing packages I offer, please visit: http://www.resumeaustralia.net/services.

Search Jobs

I work with various recruitment partners who are often seeking overseas professionals – whether they already have PR or are looking for employer sponsorship. If you would like to join my mailing list so that you can receive details of jobs that I have available, please visit: www.sponsoredjobsinaustralia.com/category/sponsored-jobs.

Professional Migration Advice

Would you like to get some professional migration advice to confirm what your available options are? If yes, TSS Immigration offer reasonable rates for assessments and for visa application assistance. I regularly work with Will Aldous, a MARA registered agent who is friendly and helpful, and whom I recommend for migration advice. Will is a very busy man, and can only assist people wo are serious about migrating to Australia. If that sounds like you, make sure you add "Referral from Nadine Myers" in the subject header of your email to ensure that he prioritises your enquiry. Will can be reached at: will@tssgroup.com.au.

For all other questions, please feel free to contact me at australianjobsearch@gmail.com.

About the Author

"Defeat doesn't finish a man, quit does. A man is not finished when he's defeated. He's finished when he quits."

- Richard M Nixon

Nadine Myers is the Founder and Director of many of Australia's leading job search assistance websites, assisting locals as well as migrants from all over the world to successfully secure employment in Australia.

Degree qualified in Business Management through the University of Queensland, Australia; Nadine undertook further studies in Organisational Psychology, gained through the University of London, UK.

Now with more than 16 years' work experience gained in Australia and Internationally in Human Resource Management, Recruitment and Job Search Strategy across several industries; and around 8 years focused on job search for foreign nationals; Nadine has well and truly earned her title of *Australia's Emigration Job Search Strategist*.

Nadine currently runs www.ResumeAustralia.net, www.SponsoredJobsInAustralia.com, www.NadineMyers.com and www.FindJobsInOz.com; as well as LinkedIn Group, Employer Sponsorship Australia (http://linkd.in/1ixncLP) and Facebook Group (www.facebook.com/pages/Nadine-Myers/599139263538076); is author of several books on the topic of job search in Australia and has been featured twice in Australian & NZ Magazine, UK. Nadine not only assists locals and emigrants to prepare their CV and cover letter for the Australian job market, but also provides job search strategies and techniques to help people find jobs in Australia through the hidden job market.

In her spare time, Nadine is an Australian wildlife rescuer and foster carer with a passion for nature and animals. She lives a simple, self-sustainable lifestyle off-grid in the beautiful countryside of northern NSW, Australia with her partner, chickens, cats, dogs, veggie patch and whatever Australian native animals she is caring for at the time.

CPSIA information can be obtained at www.ICGtesting.com
Printed in the USA
LVOW10s1430250416

485215LV00051B/2369/P